meadowlark west

MEADOWLARK WEST

Philip Lamantia

City Lights Books
San Francisco

Cover: Aerial view of the Colorado River (*Die Welt von oben, Munich 1966.*)

Library of Congress Cataloging-in-Publication Data
Lamantia, Philip
    Meadowlark West.
      I. Title.
PS3562.A42M4   1985   811'.54   85-29126
ISBN: 0-87286-177-5
ISBN: 0-87286-176-7 (pbk.)

CITY LIGHTS BOOKS are edited by Lawrence Ferlinghetti & Nancy J.
Peters and published at the City Lights Bookstore, 261 Columbus Avenue,
San Francisco, California 94133

For Nancy

Table of Contents

Meadowlark West

ISN'T POETRY THE DREAM OF WEAPONS?

The impossible is easy to reach
Who knows the way out of the labyrinth?
These are not rhetorical questions
the heart has its reasons though reasons not
                    Imaginary
the postmodern world has faded today
tomorrow, well shucks, it's here
a wedding calmly observed between heart and head
Relax the slow confusion flows until
the tooth of it
forgotten on a summer beach in Southern California
the way it's drawled to death in Southern California where death is
   cozy and Lemurian
Today I had my *tamasic* enlightenment the federation of anarchs was
   conspiratorially formed in Albania
the news came by indirect means the lines were jammed but I think
   I got it straight
here in the Far West you know how hard of hearing we are You've
   heard tell Ah'm sure
the clay hands looking a little moldy of Joaquin San Joaquin
the lazy simple status
nowhere to
and
always AND
Can this be the surprise statement
      Nuub
            nuub
                  with high rhetoric back from bright death
what else to say of it?
No luck a metaphysical symbol
There's soaring even among the tortured minerals

These are the gilds of free verse
Doesn't the horror of writing Am I reading?
Better not to repeat you Sovereign Powers
the astral too plain at noon black with engines slipping again
five times
the secret hoarded afresh
Look at the basket now, my friend, *where* the fruits among the froth?
Between the ecstasy and the secret
I've touched bottom I want to be lost
the glow is bathing me in pain
the master would say, *souffrance*
Cosmic recurrence of the light of the old
its youth becoming
planting Dada on the trees
The within is without at once
no sooner dead than living
the unique perspective dangles the motion
it was called the boat of Ra
and the golden night hermetically sealed
            pure rollicking play
hands are glowing the last look back
lighted shadows like video
the words you see
pomegranate of idea
a pile of rust
Poetry knows in the unknowing
but *Kemi* is the moment to send up the aroma of dragons
beyond the limits salt of the sun
the deliberate anomaly willed by nexus
covers the filings I remember to forget dead to the sun
                  Nescience
the sandpiper's ignition
Illuminate manuscripts explode through glass

your behemoth or mine
the salty bowels of Satan no less a shadow
the aquarian *pied-à-terre* this crocus of glittering mud island,
    the grebe's look, diving
transmutational obsidian
between Mount Konocti and Shasta
            across the boat of the sky people

But for love
there were new forms to birth
life was not
but for life only begun
among the various gleamings, light bearers, I met one and there are
    others at the heart of the mineral subject
It's the irrational factor
unraveling out of sight Joan Crawford at the heights the snarl
    of Dorian Gray *Comedia* of sleight of hand the velvet tissues
Watch the bean
                the Marvellous
in the wisp of wind rounding the corner at Carabeo where the
    magician had set up his rectangular table, hand and eye in the other
Today tropic birds in winter overhead as if I knew something
cubicles of wandering sound
wild parakeets to the lighthouse on the hill
This is the dream of the supernatural land
from rocking to it, what was once pain
is the bliss of it
The green demons with silvery genitalia rain down the flags of
    omnivorous pines
                dilating light

NATIVE MEDICINE

Forty years ago I was born from a crumpled tower of immaculates that
 twist like the fleeting damaged bridge torrential rain on a road
 nearing Chehalis
                          love driving through her native land the beauty
 of all I've received from her
the tears of an erotic Amonite sail Puget Sound to exalt the forest
 spirits we for whom all was Coyote made
the moments at Daladano our home in transfigured space
When I say love of the land I begin with native Amerindia:
Ohlones, Miwuk, Pomo, Ramytush, Salinan
with the Washo peyotlists from the morning prayer in the bowl
 of dawn
none shall ever steal from me our sixty eyes to the smoke hole at
 the Tipi flue
embers of sacred earth—the myth has not lied—
a poor man like they—old in the vision of the floating tipi over the
 hideous towns below—once with the gods they say—but I'm no
 metaphysician, stop short at the crumble of dogmas—
the objects are prefigures of omniscient dew
the slash of cosmic jokery
corpses of the doomed sciences light the way against the rhetoric of
 anti-rhetoric and human misery true fault line of Birdy Dick 'Old
 Grandmother'
I send up the song I could not sing this land my stony prayer people
 of human misery
Repetition shall not make it less than our hearts entwined
I am your mystery as you are there among the Pleiades
Ancient ones only you shall see us through
Serpent of suffering
they say there is nothing higher in the black grackle sounds at nightfall

     Spumes

4

TREE

The slab of secrecy Wordsworth rays with remembered light
  the luminous forest of wakened subjects birds weaving his words
the voice of *El Señor* the cape in the umbrella of voices
exchange of crowns on the watery steps Never Before intricate
  movements of subliminal audiation, fade-outs in the fabric of words
  the laryngeal vibrations of the crow of thought
fading steps to language
a few sparrow notes in the dense fog
a heraldic demon of the moment
Exactly perhaps perhaps exactly
it rains horse pearls of *anglais* from Alert Bay
the seething pit on the cubicle to strain the bit
Old pony
from the antediluvian age has carried man from the beginning
  to the end if only a shadow now
the eyes of ka-ka
                    in the circle, their ten eyes glowing
with the clay figure
the old ones on the polished abalone shell

SURREALISM IN THE MIDDLE AGES

I'm eight years older than Artaud when he died
For thirty years I've looked on the world he said consolidated in 1946
It's still consolidated, but denser. 'Enough, you charlatan, you hangnail
    vampire, the phantom above all
only the phantom, I don't want any doppelgängers in my stadium'
The mountain ridge extends the eating and the metabolic metaphors
    why not rhyme?
obscene photographs are burning like lava from Mount Rainier
'Surrealist? ... Man, we don't like those labels, yeh don't have to label
    poetry ... it *is,* man ... '
Me, I'm preromantic. I'd as lief roll up a leaf to Lady Day as anybody
the blessed clichés in sight of the tower
'a': the winter scape ghost eggs in the pan
the material image static on the Ohio River
the breasts of mounds nearing prison
pit of the world cycle sudden illumination
the coiled dream door
hungry snow cycling the land of earth's horizon
an afternoon with Osiris in the *stellae,* scorpion at hand
Masterless, the enigmas seep out of the air
on a roundout without memoirs
to red ribbons the wind-scrivener wheels to ancient storms
medusae in an optic dance
metallic blue hats across the bar
loup-garous back from the tropics
Scott Joplin's ragtime and a faraway land to the Natchez Trace
murder as only euro-americans can sing it
a slice of wigeon's tail against the timbers waiting at the bend
    of the river
great flyway of ineffable seasons

Mississippi echoic spangle there's the sea it can only be the Columbia
    or the Klamath
loon loon I see the pelican clear
Violent Ocean (another name) Pacific never

pulverable dunes of the Least Sandpiper

WEST

So the atomic apocalypse has re-arrived this time borne on a scalding
    iron with curlicues of *musique*
the Age of Bronze is the whole future-dream rainbowed with festoons
    of resurrection
south by deepest west impales the nuclear holy of holies besotted with
    dust and oil lesions rancid beetles black among the reds
coherent waterfall
the best is lunacy stress points humanity spores in ringlets of anxiety
random mystery at some black hole
chalk-lined figures run and dance through dunes of birth
an erosion of worlds
the cosmos in a nutshell of dreams that attack
at high velocity with plain chant Barbizon school of art 1930's
    Big Band Jazz and
slides out of view 'Mutilation Baby' the birth of the light

*

Salt survival glistens in raindrop third eye Polyphemous-thoughts
    graze Whether the head clears off this field of key-lined space
the torpors of harmonia
the joker leaps at the hole
from which werewolf unknown the speeding frozen fire tropics travel

At the Cafe Paradiso the glass of mineral water on the oldest rock

*

There's no worship in the temple
the hermetic secret floats elegantly among the muddy images
'I hear you diamond, drum, beat on the hill of stormy stone faces

with the end of *technē*'
The mind is a black hole of beautiful chance encounters
as with André Breton *the* André Breton in whom Jacques Vaché *is* the
    seminal gesture
Birth of the revolutionary rose
Sirens at doorways on rocks in place of gutted rooms
All the beauty of woman implied by the secret gnosis
Imagination at touch of silver flasks as they open the forest traveling
    the stony river's need

*

The villified mathematic
foam current rolling oceanic lips
eternity's veil intricates of fading geometry
To imagine Luis de Góngora y Argote advancing on the Segovian plain
    with all the horns of his third eye
the poet of *Soledades, Polifemo y Galatea* at the storefronts of
    El Duque de Albuquerque
Oraibi of the next ten thousand years

*

Crab gore To give capitalism its due duck-cracker the head of a
    christian fart
graveyard of sanctimonious filth
Overkill, the throat of the gipper the chief of the team loaded with
    scrotums of black babies
Neptunian highways of dungeons etched from the colorados to the
    shithouses of their gory southlands
Reverse gear, I'd balloon evaporate on the raging horns of the
    Marvellous the engine's vulcanization of the clerks of reason,
    the forced sodomies rammed with a sauce of fried bankers into
    the vast brilliants of the social liquidation

*

It's transparent sense: goblins gallop rills
Beneath, mankind prepares its suicide
Since 1910 the signature of angels O demons promised only Death as
    in the tarot deck
Morta-doom fleshed out on the morbid sky
leathers of psychonic enigma spelt out under the draining Ocean
drained to scarlet wood
the millenarian nightmare from which humankind, the above-man, the
    flowering of higher man, within, beyond the Nietzschian a-rhythm
Dionysian mandrakes coeval with the transforming sea, the serene
    eyes of Pelé in waters of the West
Oneiric Ocean, there's a sense through Cimmerian clashing gates
a chance in the golden sluices
above on the marshlands of being succotash and flying wormwood
spliced out on the apocalyptic nuclear wastelands
But the becoming of humankind lodges frozen limousines—1930
    scissorbacks—to Freud's dream book
the mote in the real shaking the dust of coattails Madrids of Gothic
    dust whose sinister cities re-open the superchargers turned in under
    the seat of Toltecs and human pits
as if the Ranters, at perilous roosters perigrinating fields, tuned the
    transforming card's magnet west
to the Lemurian crest
                    Anna Anáhuac
Antillean to the coracles in seas of Dream Raven Pelé
Hypnos belly the leviathan-squirrel jumps in the grass of the dead
    humus-machines of the marvellous Rosicrucian Heidelberg in front
    of the Thirty Years' War

*

This infinite reference to the external world
laid out bare bottom from Vasco da Gama
to the Mississippi slung on a wheat loaf in Kansas

1) the articulate wonder hanging over gretchen woods woven in
   pretzel of pop dreams
   spun of the lost seasons
2) the turbulent West always receding dream more than vision's
   damask
3) the baroque madness of Columbus from the ropes of Thomaar
   glistening in Shaman's burnt fetish
4) the fire stone knit with the waters of the West

*

The ring-tail of an Arcimboldist
and the genital history of this wrench
                    the clove's dive peanut of
the wing-tail of an Arcimboldist
even then the deluge myth universalized the fanciful lore of bat enclaves
   a sauce of thunder and bluebearded photons curl on the tanoak
   sidereal convulsions of Molino's 'disentanglement' of the pneumatic
   sponge
webfoot out of gear on the lake's rudderless voice *over there* in lands
   of ancient *chiclé,* mouths but mouths the bizarre traits that lead
   back to the
hangnails of an Arcimboldist
like parapsychic semblance homunculi of Absent Life
morbid delights
angle of quotidian flying glass framed up in a core of magma

Talking antlers gesticulate the coming on waves of the King of the
   Western Isle
his tree-lined face seen from a beach at Fort Bragg

SHIP OF SEERS

The dust of intolerable social conditions packed like melting bombs floats the grease of the human condition. The crystal tones form your face, Lady Urticaria, waking up in a dream of yellow jacket hives. Fixed explosive in a clash of bull horns ... recurring portraits of the dream work gleefully watch the cannibals eating the Europeans. But for your exits of shattered glass, the stage magician's hand turns up the joker tuning the valves of twentieth-century wars. Political torture machines fornicate over the frozen mire, electrical beds rain down engraved stones siphoned by arks on the waves, luminous shadows of the invisibles. There's the glint of plural worlds in the play of matter, 666, horsepower to veil and rend the putrid walls.

Pluto in Scorpio—the devachanic sheen on the perceptible plane — green gloves on the trees of the Calafian summer are the minced cuckoos to end the slaughter of the beautiful beasts.

Only eyes will be horns as antlers touch in a deer dance. The mounting collage, *The Sacrileges of Jesus,* indwells an age and scores holes the death squads shall not pass.

Only man and the bird are divine. Coasting on folds of air, the White-tailed Kite meets its mate, the great sun of love, between the paint of feathers—touch in rigorous thought. The vision situates who we are like an oracle of another world. Whoever meets the sudden revel seers the earth's renewal.   From the powders of Pelé: the return of real life. The primordial ferns wrap memory's rotosphere.

The prince of birds thought himself the intelligence of wild pride, forefront of the flying objects, hoof-marked with victory through granites of language, on paths only woods in agony spare to flight— this, the raptor's alchemic sight, oppositions of delicate harmony—

harpoon of the Inuit shaman, at hand. In an ash of words, the hanging mask floats over all the fires

Oceania

Oceanic west, the husks were sculpted in your caves like the maverick Grackle

Oceania oceanic.

HAVEN ROOT

Ichabod, Jonathan Pressgang,
lutenists populate the land
firing Poe on Fort Sumter
Malacca canes replace the tobacco of the Mississippi culture
O great Chickasaw the fox clan I invent subverts gonorrheas
      of language
the sublime Marvellous at Burney Falls in the life and times of Teddy
      Roosevelt
time to plant the magnetic spheres
at the heart of the mystery the lalops in Crater Lake
the phantom boat approaching the green beams
the man writing in the masks of Lemuria
destruction of species corruption
green speech from a green stone
the green wind of green winter
the mimetic forms
on a tongue boat of lung
sun of the bottomfish beneath the dip
where water rushed the faces in the rocks
years of green reformation
green grace
and a farflung season outside *Sol y Sombra*
America is a Transylvanian outpost occulted
but sometimes visible down a lane of trees by the ghost of
      Netzahualcoyotl
Sandman from the north always the pure aroma of pine resin electric
      to the Great Tetons
the rollicking maypoles of imaginary Canaans forgotten in redwood
      dust
Out of gather silence gathers
like snare drums gushing the golden articles

federating anarchs
the jiffy solution at the unity of opposites
the rush of Shakespeare in the oblivions of Atlantis
'this rock, sir, a blind set of blinkers'

final 'em out

the black pounded face
'vut the nazis did vuz wrong'
There's too much Aleister Crowley and the vaudevilles of,
anti-visceral campaigns are waged
no quarter in the dream desert, heraldic
       ORNITHOS
              the planet Venus
penultimatics coverge
the muscular ignitions sleep Better sleep but awaken awaken then as
   'before'
an eagle dim on the horizon
          the Great Year revolves
between the close view of
THE WHITE CROWNED

INVINCIBLE BIRTH

The glaciers of cities, pits, the abysmal mysteries of Baudelaire's
    labyrinth, one can say, breast of the city
tufts of avian mystery in the sun's eye
the old street gleaming with lizard paint
to drink ecstatic
as with, ectoplasm
the first sea-wash stain
with wind sonatas scratched from an old bore's heaven

It's in this city the supreme magic is enacted
The ballplayers appear under illusionary catapults
wood impact to wood graven images scooping invisible graves
    the solemn moment of sunlight
The afternoon habits destructions of Annapolis
morbid freaks á la P.T. Barnum
Aristocratic slaves siphon the nectars of poison
I catch a fish or let it flow
hone a jigger of gin lemons sighting birds
The deep feelings are fumbling a screwtop of the heart chakra
the death of love in youth Poisons are scarves presaged by heraldic
    kites
the marsh in a tide pool of seers

the owl occulted
the kestrel darted
poised to bridge the white eagle's tilt
to the magenta tree in a heron's eye

Two meters from Golgotha spanking Mohammed
spyglass of an ancient falconer on the *parvis* of the Temple
a human esoterist secret

harbinger of erotism
wonder of thrones
the last remnants at Klamath Falls mobbed by flickers
distant loon more distant loon

In my frenzy mantic mania whatever poisons surround me
from where to where death answers with blank disdain
Ministries of wonder are death's unknown
It's marvellous the unknown spins this pen
pure monad from the dyad
the pyramid side-glance abyssed crack
echo by owls rolled in an arbor of timeless time

The celestial dome in the sleep of eternal revolt
flowers in a couplet's eye jade horses anything will do to tread in every
    sense the psychonic oracle
It must be you Ghetto City
the drizzle of grizzlies before the flood
the electric guitar on the lugubrious slopes
On hills of popping silver
city of valleys at haven's gate
Frisco before the bucks went down the leaden towns
five thousand Indigenes under Mission Dolores
Wind tube of hordes belches the stone of silence gemmed in a series
    of ecliptic yore
passing the Shakespeare seal 'it never dies' through the happenstance
    Frisco crunch
the spinner of all violence is dove
spangled floor of vision cliché after cliché
a rerun to Gallic springs on the boat to language
the glitter of green fossil sphincters of worn pages aglow
all the animal treasures and poetry goes on swelling the tides
    squandered with dew

jonquil and juniper-flung subaqueous Sausalito
the red-winged hawk from ink spots in a knot of lore
The silver curtains of the Asterean Eden flow all the fuses at the pine
    forest decembered with infamous solar radiations
the world federation of anarchs
the myth of the South American Brilliant returned from the shoals
Perishing star systems Enough of a raid on the tsetse-fly

The kestrel's armor is a woman hunting a site beside a man
    becoming bird
Donna prima the wind in their sights
                red skylarks of escape rare seeds in a covey of quails

BLACK WINDOW

typewriter heap
point point the external world a sublime slice of superfice
standing like a star over the slaughter house
the garbled language a garlic sausage to Shiva itself a texture desire
    herself all the beauty of the world in the clashing bodies, sur-
    objective poetry, the letter 'a' in folds of obscure light from
    the dream forehead of sexual sleep lost to the highest splendor
the rocks crumble
this trance with or without you
white shadow rifting the tidal chamber of children's cruelty
papyrus dust to one side
on the other, the hungry hounds of nostalgia
orchard of her mouth of peaches
on her wrist the Arcimboldist medallion of tobacco deities in the
    crocodile mimic river whose symbol outshines all the others
on the brink of indigenous dawn
clear in the autochthonic remnant
the blazing shadows on the rocks at Hopi
the lords of life rising in the age of regeneration
the *orgia* of the first corn from hollows of earth
In the desert the Sentinel embosses lucidity with geodes of geomantic
    frenzy

Everything is in the tortoise shell
I plant the foot of Crow
symphonies of squirrel magnets thrown with disdain
Past? future? the matter matters little in sight of *nigredo*
                    and the oils of ointment
putrefaction to the bridge of purification
like new wave in the arid land stymied with sphinxes

Indwelling the calcination of words
'misanthropy forever!'
a passerby in the Pythagorean legend Dracula old friend the wheels
   of your revolt from the grave have undergone torments through
   the antibiotic bardo plane
Star War syndromes hang like purple flowers and the smack of sorcery
tiny crabs of tidepool gather all the optical rainbows for the apertures
   stigmatizing the subatomic into a calm sea
When you hear my words you will see them after coming home they
   leave me
these palpable shadows that sparkle
show their sides
dance
blow out candles
grapple
diced in sand
Just now a magnet of living juice has been whirling the mental plume
and death's sacrifice on the stone below traveling the lingual stalactites
Only verbs glow on the absolute rim
Discourses of the doctors of death are the poet's chorus
                       'September in the Rain'
Turkish quarter of raspberry ice in the gloom
of immaculate restaurants a spoonbill between her thighs

AMERICA IN THE AGE OF GOLD

This one gives out he thinks poetry's at his beck and call
magic though proves it otherwise
even if adhered 'spiritually'
soul whoppers gleam like solar rain
swift beaks of spring
golden automobiles in the muse's eye
the only darkness set in the distance
back to spectral Demo rotten mythologies stifle the air
thunders of the external world internalize
'and pay them no heed'
laying out the cards of triplicate dreams
always the future ruins of Coit Tower Manhattan African cities

From this north my head is full of you, Sur America
Sor Juana sailing the cloud her back to us from Mexico *real*
meeting John Donne in Arizona nearby the Penitentes are active
the massacres at Humboldt Bay later in the nineteenth century
recall now to memory
under the ruins of Brasilia
the red obsidian light of Church's *Cotopoxi*
siphon from the black marvellous swan in glass
the way trees revolve cosmic beauty
                    Pine of diamond crest
                    warblers of dew
Oak on the swollen breath at ocean
ancient wood my native land all this that vanishes

It's Blue Jay the doctor bird under cover of the silent machines
waits in the wind of Crow Raven Blackbird
ways the language leagues to bridge the polis
                    sugar of the secessional forest city

the last utopia a mimesis like the tree monkey of Borneo
given to Mallard 'the most beautiful of the Bird People'
for the Pomo there below Mount Konocti the home of Obsidian Man
to the whisper in the waterfall
There are many centers of mystic geography
but the great Black V of gold flashing in the meadow Bird unknown
opening the air like all the lore of the chants
                this may serve as shield
for the companions of the kestrel

At the green bowls green the revels of time
to step into orbs of the before time
wake up where the glyphs are lit within
with purest golden light
the Dawn-Bringer Meadowlark
the inner temple the forest temple
the American destiny line carries us to the Klamath meeting the ocean
    the river salmon spawn
Karuk of my dreams who dance the world renewal
the pentagonic flower of spring
legends of pine warblers
Junco of the most elegant suit
in a song of dynamic black and white
                        alternate tones
harmonic wholes
                alcohols of
        the secondary powers

In the last wilderness of the mind
the chatter of world destruction below above the telepathic line
the minor key to the weather
the landscapes of Volney's ruins of empire
the expanding luminosity of Cole's Catskill paintings

I think of Cole at Burney Falls
Quidor at the Rogue River Rapids
the anonymous painter of *Meditation By the Sea* at Cape Arago on the
    secessionist coast
South channel to the riparian woods
all over Northern California still the end day imaginary land
lupines and poppies vegetable craters volcanic whispers
Wind ancient wind has hatched these Calafian landscapes
the sublime in the old sense
in the last days optic revolutions open the definitive end a forest to be
the irrational on a hindstone
Fata Morgana of the desolate strait
a hundred-mile wind and waves of violent ocean
There you drown send the death and with lumens belabor the straits
    surfaced to Shiva
She angelic tongue or not We're coming from the east to Celtic shores
    across the golden belt hanging the sights the flare of sand in the sea
    of dreams
wave of constant death the way red by chance comes forth
Antique language diagonal to intersections of time
south by northeast one with serpentine rock
warblers off nets the cliff hanger's spell
birds so caped the skies in the time of the Karkins
to walk a living bridge of salmon
what was once joy with the supernatural beings
Gilak in the Pomo legend
That these spirits are here now with the clunk of material letters
the yellow-billed Magpie in the dry wind

Old nights of Bisbee the parades rolling back to Frisco
the Huachuca mountains inflected in a grossbeak
Copper blue rim of the rambling planet
across the *collini lombardini*

1985 a number of antique
printout somewhere primitive
countryside of
imaginary birds
Who can knit you in a closet?
The onrush of the western mythic image minute luminist transcription
subverts the language the Canadian octophagic sails out of sight

The leader of a band of criminals
old Murrel It's good enough to skewer the waters
of the Natchez Trace There's sympathetic survival
early nineteenth-century outlaw of the wilderness
'Murrel's the finest'—'a wit of the wilds'—'a poet of predatory powers'

There's nary a Wilson but the warblers send cascades that wing
    the ears of Choctaws
Poetry magic love liberty
the unequivocally mediocre is an anti-meditation on bird houses
golden ringlets rare afternoons
the glade of theoric ornithic hermetica
a talon of deva dravidian bird
dæmon of legend
plucking the string
a diagonal of dew for the finches red-streaked
for the blush of the sun
the fifth note

WILDERNESS SACRED WILDERNESS

It's cozy to be a poet in a bed, on a copse, knoll, in a room
It's terrible to be a poet dragons around to bite off your wings and
    dream of the Standing One
as Nietzsche turns into Victor Emmanuel Re di Italia
Helen Ennoia looks up into the eternal pools of the eyes of Simon
    Magus
and all the botched lies of mythic ties kick open the corpse
    a bag of museum dust
                  manikin
in the manner of Simon Rodia, Buffalo Bill, like P.T. Barnum like
    Alka Seltzer
              goes against it
burnt pork eaters
El Dorado is the flashback to pancake mornings 'home is where you
    hang yourself'
             signed Bill
The games of golf on the misogynist wastes
centuries multiply metaphysical field notes
There's the sleep of Ra in the West
a blurred photo of purple and lumens
on a windy hilltop in the manner of Man Ray
luminous sky my own poetry chimes at the horrid hour of hideous
    chimes
Poe's Appalachia in the far western sea where the forest saves us
    the forest hides us telepathenes in a circle of friends
salacious hour of shadows regions of the undead
hangnails of the Gilak an infinite crystalline substance spun all the
    traditions
moored in nine powers the gurgling carburetors
the video cassettes the people are coming we're at
the communion on the mountaintop it's true but

the wheel turns the beaver chews the pole holding up the world
It's coming back home like a dream-memoir at the death of day
    in the poetical pastiche framing a mask of postcard view from
    the dawn of Ra
it's the moment of Maldoror
the collage objects of the end days conjunct the plutonic week a
    roadshow of nineteenth-century bison
as the Buffalo Bill Follies autodestruct by 1916

SWEETBRIER

No time like the present to damage the brain
at the hoodwink of nuclear physics a lamentable science
the red-faced cormorant on the rocks through the filaments of original
    creations at Fort Bragg

Precipice of a lost floating object of deciduous funnel
sighting the common merganser
From the prevailing temple a xylophonic rendition of concordant
    Symplegades
triangulated to the harmelodic pentagram
seven disks of seven depths
with a mirror transcribing Mount Hood
the erosion of redwood graves
the sufite mysteries multiple worlds (you've heard it before)
a majestic earthquake Los Angeles-style the forefront cranial thrust
It's 1879 I'm crossing the Rhineland
laughter in a glass of bilge water
the crust of the frolicking wood
hands off the waterfowls!
a little creep noise obeisance of slave enigma
oyster catchers with orange tourniquets
(cut the nonsense—no—emphatic yore of lore—bring it about,
    Burgundians!)
with a clip of Edward Lear
my fork of splintereens
gull ladies on the fleeting deck
macho voices flail lambs at gurgle obscenity

the gulch rococco pinnacles
there the birds land

a violent tradition glides by the heart of those rocks I live
the last time round a spore war

nowhere to go to see to be to crimp

*

It's nighttime in the wigwams of the West
(there never were any)
There were tree houses and lean-tos
the link to the antique esoterist oak
millions of Squirrel Girls in manzanita
only the lucids of luciferian dew
Yeh-ho-wosh-ohey-yah
the astral interludes
motorific cyclones a bridge of garnet almost granite
the prediluvian sand
no more infinity
a sulphuric sun of cement
no more time
mirror that reads me
turtles and the *roi du monde* to garner waves womb and Anglo-
    Norman relations
power of dream sonnets Piccolo above the powers
rites of the mechanical man
the green restaurants of his slow-motion grace
leaven to the Celtica renewed Martin de Pasqually to Saint-Martin
    two hundred years
from the reintegration of man
You've got it I am Mount Shasta Also acid rains

*

At tungite
oil beams coiling Lombard Street
the medieval tomtit rare sighting
a coracle of repellent forces a snipe
There's the grand sentence
oriole wrappings over the hound dog mouth of *poesis*
It's time for frickle frackle
glut of virus
the voice of klunkies in the street
my friends the Blue Jays of *paradesh*
the juggler veins of jungles
beached out the entrance to the dream curtain
imperishable myth and the slip out of dream figures in an irony
Close-fisted volcano
slow reams of clashing bodies
harmonias of silt
fog monsters the quadruped renewals of lark
we live in the north of the Gilak's Land
It's the solar magic of the place
swifts starlings cabal on a plane of pitfalls plots the polis-pears and a
    hocus-pocus hand tears from a Twenties poster generating the rose
    of the winds
pale cloth of reformation on the far western shore

Treasuries of hummingbird preserves sequestered against the vegetable
    ogres
perishing dolmens
silt of gold gulches
the wind-spread of velocity's gale
vulcans of Ocean far western rookeries and phantom birds

THE ROMANTIST

Western winds from Oceania and the dream of sighting the great
    singing thrush
wings dart the sword in hand on the crest of the Duke of Calabria
all of this which confounds 'cabala' with 'gabalis' and the Immortal
    Cagliostro
the power of *Chi'i*
erotism denuded of its chalks
off into morbid matter the flung dozen puncture the Smokies
eagle heart swallowed on the Rockies of icy dreams

Ornithos looms

with sunlit shafts of western isles
whale challengers over the driftwood gales
dreaming the birds of Borneo and the great
vulvic breast of Mount Rainier

        rituals worked by material substances
the powers of bedrock across the lichen-headed toads
of powers, dimly they say, the massive unnecessary pain heightens the
    White-tailed Kite and favors Aurora
the pith in the crack of the secret lore
    a Punjabi more or less sacrosanct
        bilge in a faun
Elemental animists mount the surrealist card of Pancho Villa and the
    supreme *independencia* of Simon Bolívar

but the hideous chimes
children we dreamed the bells of Edgar Allan Poe in the school bells
    the trajectory to nightmare the broken curl of day dream
        waterfall of jugular veins nazi hips and the lichen-frenzy of

church bells
the cloud of Poe's poem seeded in the present clutter
of revivals of Lovecraft's
seer of the sepulchres of bells the flocks of reason mimic the gongs
    of all the bells
Enter the Queen thigh bones wet with moons

Fleeting dizzy with death
the lugubrious pianos dim out the song of star wars
the fleeting regenerative revolutions to the source
the Great Blue Heron intersects humankind on the path to the stellar
    obscurum
Forever is a day forceps of mind
melted glacier churning truth the lies on time
sudden eclipses
the rent run of national bejaysus gabble history
a strand of ritual teeth the author of *Maldoror* precurses the swift's
    mandible at the close of the century the blooming trace of Robbie
    Burns vindicating woman
the rite around the oval, planes air
a crowd of anarchs
liebe Silvanus love and mysteries
a glade, deciduous temple-scape
junk food spit loggerhead to Merlin's maze
                seeds
of funny cataleptic electronicals nudge the licorice ball a female of the
    lunar species the black
sun of dreams that swallows all

I'm back from *Kemi*

there's an edge with wings solstice calm bracts of ashen rectangular
    dew

the hanging ovals the cream of oasis
May peppers popping Whittier-scapes through Chicago's brown dust
sentinel of wind at Surrealist Street
white houses crumbling Manhattan
and the ranches thereof

The smoky snow of me nostrils the lame deer hung with sunrise
silver snake up the rib of the Pawnee prairie at the discovery of black
    holes Chippendale with scrumptuous barracudas

                        muse of the day
all the pleasures *á la Fourier*
                    the spinning rose of eglantine
            terraces of cherry-passing rites of cedar waxwings
in communal regeneration with the forest of cities
    a twig crystalized to scavenger birds
black-horned suns in the glen

The bird landed the flower spoke
poetry is for birds
all voices clamor now lightly
a broken tool, spadixed, mumble at the torn edges
to dream awake
porous rocket of roving
members of our band
old-fashioned chloroform sends up the theater of new cities

Embarcadero trance-conductors a slip of hip

the wavering bunch angulate their eyes move in morbid costumes

ash tomb of light
romantists reap the swirls between the glances of robots
this time of sibilant rhyme

REVERY HAS ITS REASONS

'Operis processio multum Naturae placet'
'Nature takes great pleasure in the processions of the colors'
this thought from the book *King Hercules* illuminates *la noche oscura*
at the time of dangerous catastrophes tipping the scales by tortuous
    labyrinths traversed by misspelled messiahs the christian communist
    descent to the final pit and only then the chance operation another
    species transmuted to the quick conversion of liquid to the Age
    of Gold
'The Oak and I are one' said Taliesen
(the oriflamme will not work, ogre of washed-out valves)
to go off the traveled road
the cells leaves birds frankincense tour the corners of the glyphed
    theater of the walking feather river
Heat the secret longer moot point
leaving the livid solarity at the beehive's mouth
the sap explosions of honey enthuse the wood
intervals of the durational image
suckerpit of illusion taking up the reins of magic
horsing around the sacred whiskey, *'Yo soy marihuano'* wrote
    Barba-Jacob
There's a laugh confounds the door to assimilate husks boiled up
    from crystal
ice links the sirens in a glass of soma

There are no antinomies, *Masau,* in your secret room
From the fissures of Walpi you can clearly read the age of the colored
    corn
species variant lingual upon the forms
the secret thought of an ancient site
Golden Gates speeding the Pelé-lined warble Igneous Polynesia
Always I see the three-horned head to count thirteen cones rainbowed

to stalagmites off Captain Cook the fetishes of elephantine animals
    crossed by libation and pleasure at the roots
It's the skin of shadows, ornithic rites
a pulchritude Raven approves Coyote frolics
        madrone berries, miraculous *convivio*
            the final sublime on the carnivorous floor
'The right to be lazy' continues all thought
Only then the pure dream
scallop shell intricacies
singing up the spring migrations a telepathy wandering before
    returning White Crow
Night and day your head in a tumble spin of circulation

VIRGO NOIR

burning heart of love
open wound of being
through the crystal palace under the waters of Madumda

go the light body
at Mount Shasta
a sprinkle of fools
with spiritual fascisti
General Ballard into the golden Tetons
semen dripping the teeth of Saint-Germain
in his role as the abbot of atheism
Human waves of Cairo meet the ponderous faces at the Calafian coast
She's in their mouths
    a house like a pyramid
    built with rectangulars
perfect pear of a diagonal
down to the stars picked from photic jargon
The hand that writes is worth an empire on the moon
elbows on infinite plastic counters
a crashout to impressionism
flute in the mingled feet—a way out of Dolores Hidalgo
'El Español' at the end of the road visions
the sky of black patches
Twelve blazing candles
on the road to Dolores Hidalgo
Corpses with bloody worms on the road to Dolores Hidalgo
They say there's a world outside me but I know better
Enlightenment in the *kali yuga* is a daily recurrence
shubahdu it's over taking a long trip to the stars
waves of *ta-meri*
gums up to it—shaky—dracula—up under it

the beauty of it tilts the aromas beyond the gargoyle of spume
    unknown in the still sea of years aeons before in the after time
beautiful evil only you are beautiful
in a potsherd
falling through embers of sleep
to spell out the pit without mouths
but a tongue salty lepers sibilate the false bards pontificate Elysian
    dust off Mission Street
In the Far West all the birds fall *sinistre*
rise of triple towers
solely the ancients
the blue gash of manzanita
joy of the revelers passkey to Neptunian depths no surface baboon
    can smother
orbit of faery spirits on the green scum
       silvanus erectus
the phalloi swung like a boomerang in groves of clitoral ferns
green in thunder
woven neat over the glossological floor

IRRATIONAL

On a hill in Frisco
the gothic spread of the mantle
Pelican fragments
through the black port
of a species speaking stones

It will be another earth, parallel earth, in ancient states of
becoming—igneous, mineral boiling seas of other earthen worlds

But this one, once called 'the new world' is again the old world of
ancient earth, all the more living from the neural feet of vision,
Vesta the giver of forms

The return of the ancient earth is America in the gothic art of its
name, *Armorica—Hy-Brazil*—ancient Americas rising like hieratic
light in Thomas Cole's Hudson River painting

as in the Hopi cosmos and the alchemical visitation
the earth within the crust we tend
to the sidereal maps of its seas, luminous shell over the sun belt of sky
for those who fly to the sun
This old earth this old America is beginning to smoke the *krita-yugic*
paradise, the Age of Gold

As poetry is wedded to silence
the last word heard is the gold of silence the ancient earth is weaving
the humanisphere is turning
landing dead on arrival
the seances of poets Poe Blake Whitman
Emily Dickinson Samuel Greenberg
Jones Very above all

GAME'S THE RIGHT TITLE

In all the mermaid taverns of the world
his master's cap was tipped to the dregs,
the wayward leer of seers
draped another drudge, Beelzebub's bracken horde.
The floating gentlemen souped her briny breasts.
To the west from the west the ships knelled at heart's DisEase.
Knocked with frenzy
the lintel's song and the scent phoenix
piebald on a bait's long scallion—formed.
Let it go, the brangled leap,
le grand pas on a moonlit eidolon
the ricochet between pinball mouths,
rerun to Reason
digging the dank stone rizzled with reason.
Flayed on a corpulent bed of the irrational,
the open diphthongs dust the scholar
but the hated voice, become lovable with skeletal horn
to tear up the debris.
That's the light, the hand that writes
quicker than the eye, no escape from the triple stone.
Angel risen, beaten from the streets
optical illusions are my meat.
The grindstones of reality are crept with learnëd gnats,
but out on the tundra
the first-sung sparrow's song:
      a painting that windows the coming dawn
in a past so present the future tumbles to the lattice
platforms of dew. Spaced with fluorescent modules
the fact is, hate has molded love to be free
which coils around the sighted tree:
Fair Child or none. 'Cut the tree!'

the hawker's shriek. In a bobcat's dream,
Egregores from the North meet casually
at the foot of Mount Shasta
that mysterious scape of fading newspaper headlines.

WORDS I DREAM

A gem with a head
a life on the brink
falling like a lute
through endless space
heart strings are felt
the wonderous look of invisible fish
drunk as sober is
the street a dream
no dreams in death
the outside inside
and the tediums of insufferable labor
Captain Stalin in Generalisimo Franco
believe me 'the turn of things'
nightmare in a glass eye
smooth and simple as Milton's dictum
Sensuous spirit
the Babels of violence
I'll say it with sputniks and spuds of desire
on the loamy earth of the heart's desire
for the grandeurs of absolute equality
There's permission of persimmon
lore of my time

the gravitational pull of passionate wavelengths
a crack on the horizon
The fireworks of nostalgic festivals in Mexican villages
soothe the footsteps
up the city beneath the sea

PHI

'mystery of every day'
nothing has been written over nothing there's the title for the
    swan's game
there will be written never spoken in the horniest glade
forces are moving It was never done
There's the foam of its nothing that was never written heard in a gong
    without lips to speak it a horn it was peeking through X
the matter at hand
on the fire of the expanding cortex
there will be death there's no death in salt the lovers coalesce
never known how not to conceal
and yet light grows to a fifth seal
the rumpling waves of what is written
the pure blind beacons are the focus to the dream forest
to be read that has never been written

THE MARCO POLO ZONE

the way vital power dances the old hills the fabled
rivers of gold
seeping to summer eruption of gullies like phalloi in a windy city
    future ruins pucker
lost languages reborn on a crystal drop of lingual bliss
The sage-outlaw brain of heroic powers tosses the metalic labyrinth
    chewing Methuselan myths mixing alcohol pepper haunches a
    deliberate scheme to saunter the avian anarchia
I shall outlive insanity and mark the spectrum
zoomlens to the treasure
pennant-cults among barrels of squid
            electric odes
Belladonna of Atlantides
Die dreams of death and pain
die forever 'glorious militarism!'
The red-shafted flicker flames redolent fungus delirious stones
phi-tonic
let poisons thrive elixirs to be

all mouse of thigh bone
flexing pleasure pharyngeal automatism watches
Violinic triumph, *du temps,* the midgeon-eaters swimp the muffets
    of glee flayed by cotton mill workers on strike the burning
    cathedrals of ten thousand years smile on Pan
ligni-neo-logo 'permission granted'
I am lore bundled of crow dew finger of pine eaglet bone of my bone
    soaring thought
It was the witch of Endor
faeries like rock clusters
key of putrefaction of all possible worlds
feet below concrete terra bones crunch underground

the green solarities phanic masks
     pituitary phallus
          walls of tumbling history tiny hands waving from windows

this is no wind but hails of the West
silence the true luxury
against an auger of pain like a screaming root
linking vegetal man to Ithypallic Min from the navel returned to upper
     air of gem-lined dream of imaginable space the tooth of omnispheres
     at passions of granite and lace

                              Tum

my eyes are yours Great Blue Heron
the pleasures of writing you invisible telegraph of nature
a spent *dea* on the turning cycles
oak powers renewing the mythopoeia

Fez from the Atlantic waves of Tingis
the city that waves
donkey on the ocean
closing gates of Osirian disk
in a wandering rerun to the far western
serpentine light
muddy river at the wispy beams
the night fog comes to dream

the bulging orbs the bunches goey-oey
          cherries winging suckle dew
my tree haunch grape glow of spark nails
hot hills of hair
down the forelock
of the rumpled explosions of Shiva

the gist diadem
lost like swan eternities in an epiphany ending the worlds
Paroxysm of Coyote's manzanita berries
        all that is lost/fugitive/maddened by drugs
turns to prose, but poetry annulled ciphers another voice
the gilded deck chair in a rodent's transvex corridor publishing aerian
   copperlinks
dissolving Arizona *alchemiste*

ZANONI   A WESTERN BORDER TOWN

     sits like a gesture
     moment by moment between the afflatus tinctures
Vel Vel the grimoires are leaking
not to know the lianas interject the plausible metaphysical bridge
   to the Great Adventure
as the sands converge their colors
       scintillate the bronze morning
let the tears blacken
the fertile acids deliver the branches making a lingual fruit for the
   so-called 'gods'
which is not what I meant
fall this way or that it's the same
'That's the last you'll hear of it, de Chirico'
       the Head Man *Testa di oro*

the heave of the ropes as we sight the great unknown land

Unachieved in winter a visit to
the fault lines of earth
      my right to leave the wheel with the horned ones of the hills

pelagic birds in oilslick
at hermaphroditic play no more tray to the intermediate world

Phantoms of the mind there's nothing to it
the mediumistic bridge left open by Helene Smith continually opens
   the way 'From India to the Planet Mars'
the cacadoo of vedic dust kicks up the Silurian script
the head in the Mug sphinxed out as a choir the warm feel
   of *vox humana*
as silence enobles you diamond darkness through the terraces of being

marvellous subtle Spring of livid rocks
the merganser's tones climb to escape cerebral comprehension
the green gorgon sights the scalpel of disjunction and the instant of
   re-conjunction
Return to the forest is arduous ritual
the serpentine forms, indivisible, irreversible
Mercury
Quick
and your dumpling burned to ashes There's the lighted passage to
   the glossy-plate photos of ancient Egypt the Sphinx the temples
   of Karnak Luxor there is
no explaining it away
Luxor of the mental gesture of light
'There's nothing outside *Kemi*'
the secret seals the way it comes back to me
                    Downtown Philadelphia the angular sunset
sensorial particles
from the tip of the pyramid
at nineteen taking a sleepwalker's trip into that abyss—the abyss of
   certain poets like Lautréamont
there's a tunnel to the past that left the future
tunnel to taking hold of it
as if it were a pile of clean shirts
                    in the spirit of misanthropy

BUNCOMBE

the wounds gape out of the green cape of flimsy steel
on the hill the European tourists
are cannibalizing the gas-guzzlers of 1965
beautiful wrecks
the entry of rosy-eyed grace
tasting the juicy art of chassis-makers of the old school
back there and front chrome-goddesses and the hoods thereof
fakers of dash

put your head through this block of gores cold gores
I am swept among the trees

DEATH JETS

three of them have terrorized my apollo finger
most hideous
of human existence
for the umpteenth time, sans life

commentary   3/10/84

These lines respond to the omnipresent threat of species suicide, to
an 'eternal' moment of decision, since it is certain that the sentence
of death is passed unless there arise a conscious revolt against the
forces of death—a mutational movement in opposition to all the
moribund political powers who continue to sanction 'Blue Angels,'
whereas, thrills vaster than the poetry of Ausias March await us if,
by the next century, Betelgeuse
always Betelgeuse
pervades the skyscapes a sudden sensuous freedom to sweetly ask for
    chi'i in all moments

Are there any toxic beasts? Is Klamath Falls the origin?
Lemuria awaits its Tungsten mines florid with great masters
    Finally the gorge is redeemed
    with a sight worth revealing
accent on the plutonian age
your cipher in the markets of gloom
I'm over the borderline there are no barriers Accipiter ferries take us
    to the final solution
Are there end days in the ruins? The scandals of Cagliostro still
    ripple the curtain the Heraclitean wind effects Orbs rolling over
    Silence before dusk
Even here there's the *symbolique* of the birds Infinite tonal
    convolutions

48

the immense coil of the *Neter*—better the blur
than illucid light—better the talons will grow
as in the vegetable stone
It's prohibited to censor
A dream of birding the ancient Presidio
October when the warblers are caught in visual nets beyond the
    replica of Rodin's 'Thinker'
on the headlands
the red-shafted flicker feathers are ancient Pomo fetishes
for the Stage Magician (trees
clamoring the rosebudded chest)
soars among the mental acrobatics the Venus Torso whisked away at
    the mysteries of Anarchy
at the mysteries of Anarchy, they will deny them, the thinking Heads
    are rethinking 'the Idea' in the commune of Anarchs

I have loved only the fleeting riches
                luxury before you
shiva, unknown, a forest power
shakti and I are one among the Anarchs

FADING LETTERS

a certain attention to detail
sight of forgotten life on the wheel
       Ebony finger tip
to water the lip of Osirian dinner
China of the ten thousand dishes
To write frantically madly fanatically
like those idols the old men sold in the ancient turn of the Age
harmony winters the octaves of the shell seduced by mineral salts
glinting from spores of being
objects dart as far as I receive them
shadows of despair coil in every urban eye
rural congresses retire
dance of the Rogue River at the clashing points in the rocks

When I took off I was going to the land of poetry but I didn't know it
for a few moments I saw the enigmatic castles suited without a tie
the glow of sight
never to fade
all that divides me from it Porous lava
no one says 'boiled' with sweet vengeance the forestation of Tubingen
On the arthritic river
swallows are languorous divinities
       messages in the chipped stones
Ave caesar
pure bird
Swainson's Thrush last movements of sensorial freedom
Werewolf or not
meat must be eaten
      shiva
suture on a flyway
dampening the peppers dancing at Half Moon Bay

copper hills eating crabs eating microscopic fungi a lemon of mites of
    eyelids
the way harmony is revealed across a room night has veiled with high
    noon
I think there will be a cowboy poet at the end of the cycle
the Kid in all the Tombstones, imaginary sludge over Bisbee
nostrils on the lunar crater dying in it collectively
                the dwellers Copper, on you, dwell
something miraculous as thirst in the desert How to handle it without
    magic
the bleeding head of some nineteenth-century North American poet
    Canadian maybe French-Canadian
There's no town like Vancouver British Columbia
Poe and Whitman to the people of Raven Whale Thunderbird and the
    supernatural beings whose names
ring the ether O to see the Karuk dance Irrepressible Geograph
children laughing down a green hillock in a Spring painting
to Quidor's imaginary travel-look tails
the disintegration of the bullet aimed at the miraculous Pigeon
Robin in the aerial time of the rotten borough
the task at hand I can barely burrow but the hyacinth of the season
    A Poetic Instant
in Hegel's bacchanalian revery
back there in the old spleen chamber
modest or not Death maudlin with spring clothes
the winter sun has always been my favorite
Yes the dying sun sons of the weed to its dying madness
sparrows in the rocks of the lookouts after Prophetic Famine
all was Ra in the West
from the reeds in the transient room Mid-Earth black orbs the oars
    of the fishing boats
swarming the insects craven with red streams of ornithic talk

the Sombers were blazing lights Hummingbird octangulates summer
   with all its *chiaroscuro* doublets of dew
in the morning of Ra

THE MYSTERIES OF WRITING
IN THE WEST

Tellus old earth whose houses are perched like 'the language of
   the birds'
giants of genocide slice the shadows to species suicide
the air of the message in the old sun
volcanic oil of lime at the edge of the flame rearranging forests
the priests have rioted in the last prison
Mark Plug Stone and the radiant cliffs at Hopi
the bronze raindrop
the churning rasps of the *bohanna* strips
the legends are silent
huff out at end of the century
millenarian shuffleboard diagonal to the cybernetic cipher
hawk-eyed tambourine in a glade in Spenser's liquifying glass
   of gremlins
spoofs of the waters of Renaissance Grace
the long cut of Gypsy garb in the cigarette century
the perishing republics blown up regenerate roses in honey dip time

In the monastic life of Jack the Ripper harpoon of subarctic glaciers
   between the *teoria volcanica* and the array of forms
the ultimate species suicide by nuclear bombardment
to the slobbering emptiness
of the gyrating generals with exploded testicles
the sly crisscrosses
precessional processional
in the night wind of solar implosions
Nicolas Flamel at his cafe row
the rats of christianity void the gates west
we go
of all nights the solar spectrum is most redolent black with gold

To the fly-plinth of death
the dogmas of Clementine shackle and shit centaurs
morbid the seasalt spark
breaks in a heart-mogopolis
the windshield wiper's gamin grimace
and grimoires of
flouted flute of your embrains Lagolith a portion of the Grail
mauvey the lung-eh
          a smithy
             to flake
the formal gargoyle sucks in its sweater
sails in pockets are shells
a dream far away in crystalline shells
beggared with lichen and wind-jambs
with dentalium of worm whippers
the sooth sculptural flywheel gasconade on the destruction of
   socket-scrapers
prisons plagued to an empty card deck on the horizons of Hopland
syringes balanced by elixir poisons
goggle-grinders from livers of imaginary volition

               fly bottle on the crimson sea

                       *

Fawn of granulate stone
It's Marco Polo time in the Far West
down by the bunkers of thunder
'Move the prisms north
              the south direction is not propitious
follow the star ..'
Invisible visible the hobgoblins of light saunter past bricks falling over
   Krazy Kat

in a summer of fogs
the earth my marrow
the sponge of nothingness gluing the atmospheres
legend winds over the window of natural devices plunged in a flask of
    green venom
legends go down the drain in old salty warbles
duck farms cut up by elemental decretals
forty buckets of thorn apples
dew to the ramble in neutral
Flavius Josephus rolling the bolts to the shippers
and dim messages from Easter Island

Buenos Aires in a silver bullet fondling the diamond black hair the
    longest in the world weaving home the swan of Montevideo
    in the year 1926
the dust of Patagonia is world enough calling the spiked aureoles of
    water, cave of mental geomant, at the zodiac at the Cliff House
a little gulf of spectral sediment
home free in a bug's eye
let alone the mite's zygote of marvels
the little cone of light hardly noticed on the brink of delivery final
    matrix of sex and thunder
stand up for Reason The Sun of Darkness
all the opposites dimmed to existent chaos
the splendid wart of incipient conundrums
and the poet is born on the chance wonders of the next century
    Tubalcain returns the metals on catcalls of wandering rivers
of *poesis*

This is a land I once lost myself where the mountains cast spells
flame throwers signal their conferees below who hatch the fire-stone
A doubling of myth
the bodies roll over on the northern roads with spectral mist 'the little
    cloud'

Moana at the scorpion's lair with aureoles of corn powder
the seven years in the seven salt shakers
in the green altars of the selvas of Manzanilla
the statues become pebbles
decrying the iron-clad man truncated by thunder soaped
    in stony eclipses
the *zocolo* of will-of-the-wisps
the first night of fireworks
the sleeping loaves of terraced corn

To look into the mirror black sun in the clouds of Magonia

Even as I meditate on an ocean of mastery, the sacred herb ensorcels
    until the words of its presence concretize the momentary short
    circuit of daylight as if it were nighttime
and suddenly all is flight
little warbles of shivaite fingers cross the sea of Enigma the way of
    Inspired Gull, despised bird of deities
words on the marrow actual wing dissecting dream worlds
    the only truth

Dell flowers on rampage of graceful solutions
the morbido-suit in porcupine pleasures are man's teeth
Only the feminine unspeakable Nun bled on all the pornographs
    of noise great snot rag of the gods
their metallic heels snapt to the rhythm of the labyrinth

SPRING

In the meadow waiting for the plane to San Juan Peyotán
on the mule to Jesus María El Nayár
eyebrows of the mountain cliffs simulate the western sun
crossing *el rio de los Nayeri*
the dolmenic rocks glisten at high noon
going down the mountain to the valley of the *Nayeri*
to drink cool *jamaica* water in the warm night
dreaming of the rites that will be they were and they are and they are knitting the
    tobacco pouch by *luna*
        carving the bowl by *sol*

the aesthetic harpoon vista
        vine
a layaway
        fleeting feet
Andromeda of the birds

Paris at the beginning of the Heroic Age in the Twenties making the
    round of cafes with surrealist friends the young Breton Soupault
    Péret Artaud
time of the Surrealist Research Bureau
Amber liquors
'modern style' at the metro station
vision of another world
'end of the christian era'
before holocaust and nuclear war
nymphs and the horned men of the harvest
the winged heart which is bird
Spring on the boulevards with the phantoms at high noon
Here in Calafia Spring has returned

the Chanty Bird sings in amber street light predawn song the auto-
    matistic weaving worthy of Neith the ancient Egyptian Neter
    She Who Weaves the World

There's the perfection of harmony from Hölderlin's heart sailing
    the Bois de Boulogne
stalinist betrayals dim gargoyles in the hypnotic glance between
    Chirico's masked men
even in 1936 the Lone Ranger ravaged the old oaks to Southern
    California
the brick hit Officer Pup Krazy Kat overtook the American loneliness
the irrational smiled in Spring
the crazed war came later
We're at the foreplay of liberty
the void expands the warm heart of surrealist spring

The young poet died in Mexico taking the wrong road to Dolores
    Hidalgo
where a mysterious plague raged for months unknown to the rest
    of the world

AN AMERICAN PLACE

To have heard Moon Dog on a corner in Manhattan visage and sounds
    of Moon Dog in a video of the imaginary assault on 'reasonable
    solutions'
awakens the fool-proof diagram of antique script defying computer
    printouts
fungi eroding metal Hope the Glimmer Goddess at the platform of
    hieratic beings moving in the landscape
handing the fruits back and forth into primeval gold
all that the triumvirate exalts
milking the Babylonian computer games
shreds of lowgrade dipthongs
shady political pits only the doggerel mongers eat
reversing gear
an encyclopedia of Swiftian solutions
                      per force
the mall people conjecture
'Are there are other lives?'
In the myth of Rimbaud the living live on in the living
sons of Arto
and the companions, navigate, navigator—gold!
Oh the paling Pounds and Eliots
when I think of you, seers, Poe Whitman Breton Rimbaud Blake
Do I dare mention their names? Thelonious Monk Charlie Parker
Magritte Oelze who smokes all the old world charms
              into the woods with binoculars
              five minutes before oblivion
A dance a sacral dance a blend of harmonies baked by igniting
    redwood trees little mystery theater when it was nothing a boogie
    a wandering minstrel show of the Plague Victims
how the old got new
Before the eighteenth century

there's a furnace coiling at Ypres On the Natchez Trace there's
    the spirit of the beatific Chickasaw
to listen with my left side No only the bridge to the right brain
there's a beckoning of the roads meeting
above the plain

FOURTH OF JULY

Resin Man turned the corner of his faery palace
Decaying politick Infinite buccolics
dim boat of crossing warbler messages
bats the dawn at Rubber City whales conifered with black bears
the chief of the Karkins and friends attack the prison of indigenes
    that was Mission Dolores
like no other the art of dreaming rattles the unknown factor
morning dew from temples of compost
all that is sacred in nature
after death poetry shall have its morning of birds
whose shimmering green light baffles and prates precisely as
germinating vessels
what escapes pulses the earth's cascade
that falls upward in a multiverse of shattered shells
overhead the flesh-hangers hiding the secret of regeneration
Chang the Invincible up from the trap doors the author of Hiawatha
    with his head in his hand
This path leads to manzanita in bloom
the vulture above Daladano signs six times the avian mystery
before the berries were Squirrel Girls
the acorn giant at Squaw Rock
the Black Cat Cafe
                Sun Assassins

Shadows turn sediments ancient hills speak in the green wind

THE GEOMETRIC HALLUCINATION

ten the shadow dual infinite pathfinder autodestruct the flint roto-
   spheres Amon's secret room you all know
beaver the strews auerhahnded Hölderlin
anything transmitted at the floodgate an opal object
like a bridal suite on a stack of burning
a cosmic heap blown on a feather raping all the images of god
Delirium will brush your teeth and glue the foods away

meta-man ithyphallic shakti

there'll be gold or never be
bone the fissure intrepid with silk suckers the morbid atoms
   reconverge to open lodges encamped with a native torch
rain, her image, to berry the desert floor
flow like language in a drop of water
there's no turning back explosive blackness subverts the
pseudo-marvellous at the knell of Capital
walk-on parts of a decaying hole
The tungite given Doctor Satan veils all the flaky colors and lords of
   whimp
the baseball lost to the Pleiades the gory military buttons auger
   the time
brown wind clichés   pneumatic metals
there's the viral hook and cranny crammed up fissures of church
   steeples hosting dead matter in the Vatican's exploding tomb
   vampire monks ascend
the vedic crispies drip from burnt flesh
poets in flames to earth theories gulp nibelungs deranging Vesta
   contained biometrically in the shadow's shadow
the orange object spins the dusky shells and the mystic peppers
                              dance rivers of the true marvellous

bone of echo the solidified mask of the poet mummies fatuous prisons
  of the afterlife

Murmuring but faster
Maneuverable sidereal flow

the dark solar membrane famish the morbido stone

REACHED THE TURN

like the opening of a door
to another land a wisp of cloud the seed reels
In the ambrosial air of the cafe across from La Scala
the *visione noblissima*
                    Tameri
marvellous contortion of the *milanesa siciliana*
morbifies the nostalgic exotic
to pare to wood the ray of carnal love
space emptied of three visions in one
This way the Isisac force expands the havens
where immortal beings move
through the computer rooms to spatial mentality

things alone are happening
legends touched with regeneration
further along the end days we appear neat/clean/whistling through
                    the bones of the old indians
even to Calafia
for there was an oceanic continent or two
secrets walked the winds of Market Street
and the lost paradise a black hole

calling on the invisibles very carefully
that a signal from Mercury is a chance

                    A wind and a rain may come
                    another crack in time brings
                    the oaken feel of an ancient
                    wind at least twenty centuries old
Mother Shipton in 1991 wistful archaic
                    frenetic the very arcane cant
                    shredded in the commonweal

EXORCIST EXERCISES

With all that winds her with wiffets of glory
beneath the sloth's gaze putrid honey of the Benedictine Brother
Woman at the antipodes
feathers of dust and perfume
island of exploding beds you pucker the ingots to glow water
of the cherry hung streets
the black mud sun on your brow ignites a rhomboid cascade
the heat-won symbols gamble on your knees of eternal marble
sly locks of leukocytes
floating billboards your thighs the flocculent seashells in all that spins
    the luminous stone of sphinxian matter
the plains rising from pink columns fiery ghosts liquify
Mirror of bad taste 'sent up' by the Deadwood Dick of spectral lips
the card of Blazing Star in the slow drawers of the Far West
The loss of pleasure in the nicotine heights
straddles the dragon of omnipotent pleasure
primordial self
succulent stone
the raisins of your timorous flesh magnolia of night of day
architrave of the future
my spigot my nomenclature against the orthodox
morphomatic revolution by the lyrical swarm
the blinding sun dissolved between
Greece and Portugal

OTHER STATES

Everything tilts and falls in the molochian void
a pitch of curled fingers serrates water verbs latent bowels of concrete
    explosions the sleep of metals in the 'thousand year reich'
logos Sogol another 'god'
                     and Amor
Stretched out love underground
a horde of monsters cross floors beings frozen with cold fire
draped interstices of 'the flat earth theory'
Tellurian thought turns with a gem in a baboon's hand
                Impenetrable land
                     dreams beyond the walls in time

Laughter walks as a three-piece suit and *baba au rhum*
down to the tip of Aquarian hail
the lugger in the spindle Tamerlane and haruspex divine
the third cheese from the left at the splatter of Doges
a seascape spliced with alcohol and *khat* from Timbuctu eros again
a thousand gamelan orchestras the tree's ear any tree any ear
In the madrone forest emblems petrify green footsteps at the red
    solar disk
time, the perfume of will-o-the-wisps
The mad eye rolling across the gulch
There's nothing
the empiric fortunes by snagged processionals
and the undoing of knots by head winds circling from lightless
    machines
putrid air in the nose of the Pope
the imams nailed on a gaping face of djinns
the starving bodhisattvas stranded on a dessicating leaf swollen with
    Bon's bones
the bubu elixir swarmed by rotting refrigerators

It's the eclipse of reason
the magnet ray gun lash at the apex splashed on granites in a green
    sleep and awake with metallic grape leaves lemons of computer
    tech detecting granular orations the first chance net the golden
    forest of Elphane
sounds of lingual gorges
and water's sound as the city gorges it

The movement is spent hide-and-seek between the hedges
the words the hedges
'demon in the angeloy' (as they say)
the provisional steps of quick change
world destruction in a pluriverse
infinite perspectives in the space between forks of leaves and
    the turgid marmoset in a whisky glass
the fumbling of symbolist scapes

Excreta of writing
quick! a displacement of mobs on the throat's columbiads
blooming deserts on the rough grade to Laytonville
woodpecker shamans saunter through firs of owl mechanics
the rapid growth of horse whips against the flanks
the flanks voyaged with pearl studs
the last look back and the trays of light afar
a shake up of shoveling death
a ray of regenerative death

matchless pain on the snow-banked summer
poured out from a cascade into a jar assuming the ocean

deep in shell's castles
the lemon leaf balloon tears up hundreds of steps to Coit Tower

Bear's paw
river of imaginary rain
mite's bridge
the forest diminishes
a turn edenic at the end

wandering in a morsel of graves
flowering manures volatile with smelting ores raining away
    under *Huracán*

A great struggle to widen the gap
Another chalice of drifting metal
the flocculent chance of onyx leaves
the dark of lights between the islands secret suns in the fires of the
    night toward the Kwakiutl dawn
'Siempre Norte'
Bear Power travels streams of paper ocean
Phantoms of light scissor the scapes to drink nine rivers beyond the
    Modoc of raging woodpeckers

At world's end the jay opens the water at Burney Falls
the spinning beaks music the green phones in a gull's speed
to tip the tree with nuggets
stillness and silence behind the egret's map of vision

Saunter a paradise between the bent rods Just so the goatherds
    of menace mandibled from Pennsylvanian hills into spore wars at
    Thunder's Place
the sheep have lunged from their star paths over Alhambra and the
    curvature of convolvulus in summer gone to the brisk of the wind
    gnarled with the smoke of mummy fat irrigating membranes of
    overturned earth of the hundred varieties of Peruvian potato
the jacknapes of surprise line my vision with orchidian trumpets

the mountain ridges of cigarette paper send up the six directions of
    Mary Austin's desert informants
leaving Los Angeles stranded on a rock's erosive ocean

The patch of summer fogs screws the ears of the forest city
through the absence of bells lacerated by the onslaught on all the
    world's religions

Reversing Year

        Swifter than hunger
        Raybolt a shift of the hand
        Slight out of gear
        And a ringlet of buzzing sound
        Speed of starlings
        The Frisco of scorpions rare mirror
        Of Nineteen Eighty Four
        The multifarious spin out of graves and pyres
        Of a wipe out by water and the golden powers

THERE

on that chain of Ohlone mountains
shafts of light on a bobcat
through the thick madrones
first seen emblems that endure cupped my nine years
the great booming voice of nature
in the red bark's sloping labyrinth
who called my name
fetishes of pebbles and tabac in a redwood pouch
secret house of bark between the branches
these lights never die whose embers glow wilder
than wilderness at the beginning of words
to catch the ring of stars
                              at the still point
of infinite sur-rational flight
all was bathed in red
according to the perfection of temporal mirrors
elastic time in the gape of memory
visionary recitals in the exultant spring oblivious to the sea

SHASTA

Against the current words came looking for me, the spark which
   evolves from *luz:* youth in the wind, tugboat in the bay, pollen
   lashes the gulfs of earthquake—laughing pilot, lingual lip sopping
   mineral waves—lost Aton hurtling forests down the atomic flue.

Steady the age, moon-signed zero minus zero year. Alexander Pope
   sabred the floxgloves. Whirlpool of Ys, the churning of divulgent
   scapes, everywhere the locus of dream. A jolly pencil in the void
   spins the tissue of stone. Graveyards of redwood root systems
   flavor salt systems going up river; the sparrows of summer launch
   pyres of rain.

Shasta great Shasta
Lemurian dream island, perhaps Atlantis, scallop on the sierras,
   Hopi sovereign of animate dream, oceanic claw: Alta California
   climbs into view.
Shasta great Shasta
geography in a mystic state later pruned by seers.

The return of the mad child molester, talking to him unravels the
   secrets of the Second World War. In the alchemical legends, there's
   a certain star seen at the completion of the Work, appears on the
   silver horizon through the trail in the grove. The languorous green
   dew strokes the burning red beam. The succulent pine resin writes
   kaleidoscopes between seasons.

The roads are closed by fire. The roads end, darken. Omens thicken,
   the psychic pain of being born. Only the blue vapor endures like
   sidereal weaving at the black seed, decay in the waters of the
   equestrian sea.

From the spiritualist masses of the nineteenth century, the flicker
feather collectors were defeated in rampant raids by inhuman
hordes. Our ancestors born of the fruit fly are delusionary
landscapes founded by autochthonal forces yet unknown. Wisps
of *tankan* containing subatomic particles in the Azoth, the
climbers mask the daemons where all was created ... Transparent
does lighten the prisms, ochres and green winds converge to
interject the crossroads to the hooded figure ... Apertures open to
the Red Pepper Shaker ... Silken inner tube— dream voice—is it
you? Toxic filaments orison the radiant ebony idol.

Like a poet of the Phantom Empire, the roofer is tarring plutonian
bones. By the melting computer stations, the power that was called
up in the Fortean Society on Union Street drifts powders over the
Lombard Steps. Hidden Marin to Mount Diablo in the east, first
greetings from Blue Jay.

Rock power to the evanescent tabu-city sunlit on the leafy leather
lizard of my hands—the madrone berry-lovers unfurl. Heat
unravels the paradigm of a unique climatology of minds and few
summer days auger the flame of Grip, a rider of rhododendrons to
the north. I see chthonic man, and it's the wheel—the hated
wheel—sending up a sliver of lucent dawn arched on a sunbeam
serrating the vegetable stone: the light of her going by, a superior
earth being, her clothes blued as a tissue of incandescent gold,
something like an appearance of words—seen.

The fox spirits screech a pentacle for the fields drenched with
flamboyant flagons, the baroque from all times, and flamenco
barocco, as I leave you, Albion, gore of song: sempiternal dream
curled in clouds of seashell, putrid cupids and the Black Fathers
raping the wood nymphs of Nouvelle Bretagne.

The masked poets rise from the crumpled floor. The last aperture, reseen, glitters like a tortured cat. The flaming madrones are projecting the ballrooms of old Bisbee Arizona with Frisco *haut cuisine,* around the horns of unknown catastrophes for the Ohlones … The point is, the point is, the external Frisco scene is beginning to look like a 1928 *National Geographic* pinpointing Atlantic City, the European tourists wearing 1984 American-style, the marriage of Europe and North America, a locus of imminent sedition: Shasta from Suisun Bay north to the Rogue River; Frisco: diplomatic zone between IT and southern empires of regrettable memory

and LA-ba
  a special *là-bas* policy will prevail.

CITY LIGHTS PUBLICATIONS

Angulo, Jamie de. *JAIME IN TAOS*
Antler. *FACTORY (Pocket Poets #38)*
Artaud, Antonin. *ANTHOLOGY*
Baudelaire, Charles. *INTIMATE JOURNALS*
Bowles, Paul. *A HUNDRED CAMELS IN THE COURTYARD*
Breá, Juan & Mary Low. *RED SPANISH NOTEBOOK*
Brecht, Stefan. *POEMS (Pocket Poets #36)*
Broughton, James. *SEEING THE LIGHT*
Buckley, Lord. *HIPARAMA OF THE CLASSICS*
Buhle, Paul. *FREE SPIRITS: Annals of the Insurgent Imagination*
Bukowski, Charles. *THE MOST BEAUTIFUL WOMAN IN TOWN*
Bukowski, Charles. *NOTES OF A DIRTY OLD MAN*
Bukowski, Charles. *SHAKESPEARE NEVER DID THIS*
Bukowski, Charles. *TALES OF ORDINARY MADNESS*
Burroughs, William S. *ROOSEVELT AFTER INAUGURATION*
Burroughs, William S. *THE BURROUGHS FILE*
Burroughs, W.S. & Allen Ginsberg. *THE YAGE LETTERS*
Carrington, Leonora. *THE HEARING TRUMPET*
Cassady, Neal. *THE FIRST THIRD*
Charters, Ann, ed. SCENES ALONG THE ROAD
CITY LIGHTS JOURNAL No. 4
Codrescu, Andrei. *IN AMERICA'S SHOES*
Corso, Gregory. *GASOLINE/VESTAL LADY ON BRATTLE*
    (Pocket Poets #8)
David Neel, Alexandra. *SECRET ORAL TEACHINGS IN*
    TIBETAN BUDDHIST SECTS
Di Prima, Diane. *REVOLUTIONARY LETTERS*
Doolittle, Hilda. *(H.D.) NOTES ON THOUGHT & VISION*
Duncan, Isadora. *ISADORA SPEAKS*
Eberhardt, Isabelle. *THE OBLIVION SEEKERS*
Fenollosa, Ernest. *THE CHINESE WRITTEN CHARACTER AS A*
    MEDIUM FOR POETRY
Ferlinghetti, Lawrence. *LEAVES OF LIFE*
Ferlinghetti, Lawrence. *PICTURES OF THE GONE WORLD*
    (Pocket Poets #1)
Ferlinghetti, Lawrence. *SEVEN DAYS IN NICARAGUA LIBRE*
Gascoyne, David. *A SHORT SURVEY OF SURREALISM*
Ginsberg, Allen. *THE FALL OF AMERICA (Pocket Poets #30)*
Ginsberg, Allen. *HOWL & OTHER POEMS (Pocket Poets #4)*
Ginsberg, Allen. *INDIAN JOURNALS*

Rosemont, Franklin. *SURREALISM & ITS*
  POPULAR ACCOMPLICES
Sanders, Ed. *INVESTIGATIVE POETRY*
Shepard, Sam. *FOOL FOR LOVE*
Shepard, Sam. *MOTEL CHRONICLES*
Snyder, Gary. *THE OLD WAYS*
Solomon, Carl. *MISHAPS PERHAPS*
Solomon, Carl. *MORE MISHAPS*
Waldman, Anne. *FAST SPEAKING WOMAN (Pocket Poets #33)*
Waley, Arthur. *THE NINE SONGS*
Wilson, Colin. *POETRY AND MYSTICISM*
Yevtushenko, Yevgeni. *RED CATS (Pocket Poets #16)*